6NJ-706-1431

OTHER TITLES OF INTEREST

- Lessons of Life
- 501 Lessons of Life
- Book of Wisdom
- Book of Wisdom – II
- Book of Wisdom – III
- Golden Quotes Vol. 1
- Golden Quotes Vol. 2
- Little Book of Success
- Happiness of Marriage

- Little Book of Relaxation
- Little Book on Achievements
- Little Book on Family Humour
- Little Book on Self Improvement
- Little Book on Managing Business
- Little Book on Bringing up Children
- Little Book on Management Quotes
- What Parents want their Kids to Know
- Time Tested Proverbs from Around the World

With Lot of Good Wishes to

_____

From

_____

OTHER TITLES OF INTEREST

- Lessons of Life
- 377 Lessons of Life
- Book of Wisdom - I
- Book of Wisdom - II
- Book of Wisdom - III
- Golden Quotes Vol. 1
- Golden Quotes Vol. 2
- Little Book of Success
- Happiness of Marriage
- Little Book of Relaxation
- Little Book on Achievements
- Little Book on Family Humour
- Little Book on Self-Improvement
- Little Book on Managing Business
- Little Book on Bringing up Children
- Little Book on Management Quotes
- What Parents want their Kids to know
- Time Tested Proverbs from Around the World

THE BOOK OF WISDOM - I

to take you towards success and happiness
The best thoughts from the best men on these subjects

Stephen W. K. Tan

BPB PUBLICATIONS
B-14, CONNAUGHT PLACE, NEW DELHI-110001

© Tech Publications Pte Ltd, Singapore

All rights reserved. Written permission must be secured from the publisher to use or reproduce any part of this book except for brief quotations in critical reviews or articles.

BPB PUBLICATIONS
B-14, Connaught Place, New Delhi-110001

First Indian Edition - 1995

Published by BPB Publications
by special arrangements with Tech Publications Pte Ltd, Singapore

Published by Manish Jain for BPB Publications, B-14, Connaught Place, New Delhi and Printed by him at **Pressworks, Delhi-110 054.**

INTRODUCTION TO THE BOOK OF WISDOM - I

If we could gather all the great ideas for success and happiness, and put them all in a book, it would be wonderful.

After 10 years of gradual accumulation, I have just about done that. So here it is, all the invaluable words from the many millionaires, entrepreneurs, pioneers, industrialists and others, who are or were the cream and pinnacle of society.

As you turn these pages, something quite miraculous is about to happen. From now on, you can make all your dream a reality. You can have the best things in life. Go for it in a big way.

--- Stephen W. K. Tan

ABILITY

Until you try, you don't know what you can't do.

--- Henry James.

ACHIEVEMENT

All achievement, all earned riches, have their beginning in an idea !

--- Napoleon Hill.

The men of great achievement are, and they have always been, those who deliberately feed, shape and control their own egos, leaving no part of the task to luck or chance, or to the varying vicissitudes of life.

--- Napoleon Hill

Modern psychology now offers you a way by which you can use your intelligence many many times more successfully. By doing so you will not only conquer most of the troubles in your life, but achieve the desires that for years you have found impossible of realization.

--- *Dr. David Seabury.*

While it is true that you can get happiness and peace and serenity from being at the lower end of the ladder, it is also true that you cannot enjoy the ecstasy of achievement. Success, in a generally accepted sense of the term, means the opportunity to experience and to realize to the maximum the forces that are within us.

--- *General David Sarnoff.*

ACTION

Action creates more fortunes than prudence.

--- *Marquis de Vauvenargues.*

Inspiration to action is the most important ingredient to success in any human activity, and inspiration to action can be developed at will.

--- *W. C. Stone.*

You can think positive thoughts all your life; you can read books on positive thinking all your life; you can go to school and get your BA, MA, and PhD; you can have great ability, many contacts, and abundant knowledge – but you will never become what God expects of you until you act.

--- *George Shinn.*

This is a world of action, not for droning in.

--- *Dickens.*

Without action, a good decision becomes meaningless, for the desire itself can die through lack of an attempt to achieve its fulfilment.

--- W. Clement Stone.

Things may come to those who wait, but only things left by those who hustle.

--- Abraham Lincoln.

ACTIVITY

While one person hesitates because he feels inferior, the other is busy making mistakes and becoming superior.

--- *Henry C. Link.*

ADAPTABILITY

There is less and less chance for the square peg to squeeze himself into the round hole under today's complex, fast-moving conditions; a man who doesn't know and cannot learn what he is doing and is not comfortable in his work hasn't much chance of getting off the ground, much less to the top.

--- J. P. Getty.

If you're still doing anything this year the same way you did it last year, you're behind the times.

--- *Anonymous.*

I can't change the direction of the wind. But can adjust my sails.

--- *Anonymous.*

ADVICE

Most of us ask for advice when we know the answer but want a different one.

--- Ivern Ball.

ALOOFNESS

The man who is above his business may one day find his business above him.

---Daniel Drew.

ALTERNATIVES

For starters, I keep a lot of balls in the air, because most deals fall out, no matter how promising they seem at first. In addition, once I've made a deal I always come up with at least a half dozen approaches to making it work, because anything can happen, even to the best-laid plans.

--- Donald Trump, American Tycoon.

APPEARANCE

Nothing succeeds like the appearance of success.

--- Christopher Lasci.

APPRECIATION

The greatest humiliation in life is to work hard on something from which you expect great appreciation, and then fail to get it.

--- Edgar W. Howe.

The deepest principle in human nature is the craving to be appreciated.

--- *William James.*

ASPIRATION

A fine life is a thought conceived in youth and realized in maturity.

--- *Alfred de Vigny.*

ASSUMPTION

Always assume your opponent to be smarter than you.

--- Walther Rathenau.

ATTITUDE

Attitudes are more important than facts.

--- Norman Vincent Peale.

A relaxed attitude lengthens a man's life.

--- Proverbs 14:30.

Believe in the best, think your best, study your best, have a goal for your best, never be satisfied with less than your best, try your best, and in the long run things will turn out for the best. Always add up the best.

---Henry Ford.

It's a fact that you can't tailor-make the situations in life, but you can tailor-make the attitudes to fit those situations before they arise.

--- Zig Ziglar.

Of one fact we can be sure: those who won positions of power, who gain recognition, who performed great services for mankind, who sought and found love, who, in whatever their sphere, became fortunate, maintained through thick and thin an affirmative attitude concerning the desires they sought to fulfil.

--- David Seabury.

BEAUTY

Though we travel the world to find the beautiful, we must carry it with us or we find it not.

--- R. W. Emerson.

BEGINNING

The beginning is the most important part of the work.

--- Horace.

He has half the deed done, who has made a beginning.

--- Horace.

BELIEF

Nothing splendid has ever been achieved except by those who dared to believe that something inside them was superior to circumstance.

--- Bruce Barton.

Believe in yourself, and what others think won't matter.

--- R. W. Emerson.

Man is made by his belief. As he believes, so is he.

--- *The Bhagavada Gita Book.*

BLAME

When a man blames others for his failures, it's a good idea to credit others with his successes.

--- H. W. Newton.

BRAIN

I not only use all the brain I have, but all I can borrow.

--- Woodrow Wilson.

It's often said, 'Familiarity breeds contempt.' So it is with the respect we show for our own brain power. Everyday tens of thousands of people think original, creative, worth-while ideas only to dismiss the idea because it came from their brain.

--- Dr. D. J. Schwartz.

CAREER

A good grasp of the market is a powerful tool for the new career professional. Know which ones have bright prospects – and which ones will decline.

--- Dr. Stephanie Jones & R. Salazar.

CATALYST

Anxiety should be used as a catalyst to help you move forward to objectives.

--- Anonymous.

CAUSE & EFFECT

Shallow men believe in luck, wise and strong men believe in cause and effect.

--- R. W. Emerson.

As a man realize that he is the cause of his effects, he can cause the kind of actions that reflect personal prosperity.

--- *Vernon Howard.*

CAUTION

The art of being very audacious and very careful at the same time is the art of success.

--- *Napoleon.*

I always go into the deal anticipating the worst. If you plan for the worst - if you can live with the worst - the good will always take care of itself.

--- Donald Trump, American Tycoon.

CHALLENGE

Making money represents the same challenge for a business person as breaking records does for an athlete.

--- Bernard Tapie.

In every man and woman's life there comes a time of ultimate challenge – a time when every resource we have is tested. .....
Some people use such tests as opportunities to become better people – others allow these experiences of life to destroy them.

--- Anthony Robbins.

CHAMPIONS

All great champions are disciplined in the image they project. They become soldiers, showing tremendous power and presence in battle.

--- *Jim Loehr.*

CHANGE

The successful implementation of an idea can be a wonderful thing for the organization and you. The organization can achieve gains in profits and productivity. As the innovator, you may achieve more money, status, career growth. Yet, to win big, you must be adept at overcoming a central problem - resistance to change.

--- Eugene Raudsepp.

To improve is to change, to be perfect is to change often.

--- Winston Churchill.

CHARACTER

When we see men of worth, we should think of becoming like them; when we see men of a contrary character, we should turn inward and examine ourselves.

--- Confucius.

Every human being is intended to have a character of his own; to be what no other is, and to do what no other can do.

--- Channing.

The foundations of character are built not by lecture, but by bricks of good example, laid day by day.

--- Leo B. Blessing.

Censure and criticism never hurt anybody. If false, they can't hurt you unless you are wanting in manly character; and if true, they show a man his weak points, and forewarn him against failure and trouble.

--- *Gladstone.*

Ability will enable a man to get to the top but character is the only thing that keeps him from falling off.

--- *Anonymous.*

CHILDREN, CHILDHOOD

In the man whose childhood has known caresses and kindness, there is always a fibre of memory that can be touched to gentle issues.

--- *George Eliot.*

Children have more need of models than of critics.

--- *Joseph Joubert.*

CIRCUMSTANCES

People are always blaming their circumstances for what they are. I don't believe in circumstances. The people who get on in this world are the people who get up and look for the circumstances they want, and, if they can't find them, make them.

--- *George Bernard Shaw.*

Learn to challenge, question, defy and investigate each situation that bothers you. Greet all situations with a wise mind. Examine them carefully and you will see that circumstances lack power to harm you.

--- *Vernon Howard.*

Man is not the creature of circumstances. Circumstances are the creatures of men.

--- *B. Disreali.*

COLLEAGUES

One of the main reasons many people do not advance in their careers is the problems they have working well with their colleagues.

--- *Iacocca, Chairman, Chrysler Corp.*

COLOURS

Colours can calm, pacify and relax; they can energize, activate and invigorate. Colours are comforting, consoling and pleasing. They can heal, uplift, restore and balance. Colours speak, to those who are ready to listen.

--- Robert Holden.

COMMUNICATION

Miscommunication, poor communication, or no communication will create problems.

--- Zig Ziglar.

CONTENTMENT

True contentment is the power of getting out of any situation all that there is in it.

--- G. K. Chesterton.

Our contentment doesn't depend on what we do or on where we find ourselves; it depends on what we think.

--- Dale Carnegie.

CONVERSATION

A gossip is one who talks to you about others; a bore is one who talks to you about himself; a brilliant conversationalist is one who talks to you about yourself.

--- R. S. Zera.

Conversation is an art, and like all art, it is improved by experience and practice.

--- Sally Chew.

So if you want people to like you; be a good listener. Encourage others to talk about themselves. Talk in terms of the other man's interest. Make the other person feel important and do it sincerely.

--- Dale Carnegie.

CO-OPERATION

Co-operation must be earned, not demanded.

--- *Zig Ziglar.*

Just as a small insignificant-looking child's magnifying glass can, when manipulated properly, concentrate so much of the sun's rays as to cause a fire, so you, with your psychic power consolidated, can multiply yourself in the kind of psychological orbit you really want.

--- *Dr. D. J. Schwartz.*

Don't disperse your forces. Once occupied with a thing, stick to it until you succeed, or until there is absolutely no hope. More than once, a fortune slipped through someone's hand because he undertook too much at the same time.

--- *P. T. Barnum.*

CONFIDENCE

What is this thing that Alexander refered to when he spoke about his destiny, that Caesar meant by his luck, Napoleon his star ? What is it, if not — the confidence each of those three men had that they would play an important role in history.

--- Charles de Gaulle.

Doubt whom you will, but never doubt yourself.

--- C. Bovee.

Success is not dependent solely on our earnest affirmation, on our self-confidence, but also on the confidence of others in us; but this confidence is very largely a reflection of our own, the effect of our own personality on them. Our own attitude of mind is, therefore, the means to produce this confidence in others.

--- *O. S. Marden.*

The confidence which we have in ourselves gives birth to much of that which we have in others.

--- *La Rochefoucauld.*

Good communicators often become great leaders. You, too, can become a leader through precise, thoughtful communication. Remember: a boss says, "Get going!" A leader says, "Let's go!".

--- George Shinn.

Precision of communication is important, more important than ever, in our era of hair-trigger balances, when a false or misunderstood word may create as much disaster as a sudden thoughtless act.

--- James Thurber.

COMPANY

The energy of success rubs off when you are in its company. Successful people think successful thoughts, make successful decisions, create successful plans, complete successful projects. You can pick up that energy and use it just by being in their company.

--- John Kehoe.

CONCENTRATION

Concentration is my motto. First honesty, then industry, then concentration.

--- Andrew Carnegie.

Concentrate all your thoughts upon the work in hand. The sun's rays do not burn until brought to a focus.

--- A. G. Bell.

To make an idea succeed, you have to concentrate on that idea alone. Or if you prefer: to succeed you must only have one idea in mind.

--- *Andre Gide.*

With peak concentration comes peak confidence: watch Greg Norman set himself for a drive and the concentration is so intense that it dazzles.

--- *Mark H. McCormack on the golf Champion G Norman.*

COURAGE

Whatever you can do, or dream you can, begin it. Boldness has genius, power and magic in it.

--- W. H. Murray.

Do not be afraid to take a big step if one is required. You can't cross a chasm in two small jumps.

--- David L. George.

One ingredient I've noticed in the personality of almost every successful person I know is the courage to risk failure. To try is definitely to risk failure, but what is your alternative? To do nothing, have nothing, and be nothing. When you do absolutely nothing you've avoided failure, but you also have avoided success.

--- *Zig Ziglar.*

Fine-tuning is no longer enough. Company survival today depends on courage and imagination – the courage to challenge prevailing business models, and the imagination to invent new services, new products, and new markets.

--- R. M. Kanter, B. A. Stein, & T. D. Jick.

Courage consists, not in blindly overlooking danger but in seeing and conquering it.

--- Richter.

Physical courage, which despises all danger, will make a man brave in one way: and moral courage, which despises all opinion, will make a man brave in another. The former would seem most necessary for the camp; the latter for the council; but to constitute a great man both are necessary.

--- *Colton.*

Courage is the first of human qualities because it is the quality that guarantees all others.

--- *Sir Winston Churchill.*

In every success story, you find someone has made a courageous decision.

--- Peter F. Drucker.

A great deal of talent is lost to the world for want of a little courage. Every day sends to their graves obscure men whom timidity prevented from making a first effort.

--- Sydney Smith.

Be strong and courageous and do the work.

--- 1 Chronicles 28:20

COURTESY

I strongly recommend you hand-carry your thank-you notes back to the interviewers the same day. You may think this tedious and unnecessary busywork. It isn't. George Bush wrote an endless stream of short notes over the decades as he made his way, step by step, up the political ladder. .... If it could help him get elected the president of the United States, it can help you get a job.

--- *Harvey Mackay.*

Nothing is ever lost by courtesy. It is the cheapest of the pleasures; costs nothing and conveys much. It pleases him who gives and him who receives, and thus, like mercy, is twice blessed.

--- Erastus Wiman.

CREATIVITY

Mere experience, without the imagination to use it constructively and creatively and without business ability, is likely to be more handicap than advantage.

--- *J. P. Getty.*

Creativity cures the chaos in the heart.

--- *Tibetan proverb.*

If you want to succeed, you have to forge new paths and avoid borrowed ones.

--- John Rockefeller, American industrialist.

DARING

Often we have to make a choice between security and a touch of daring. Security is good sometimes, but a challenge also has its rewards. Recently I saw a sailing vessel with sails hanging limp and lifeless on the mast. The vessel was not moving, but sat motionless and tranquil on the slick, calm surface of the harbour. The ship was safe and secure, but it wasn't going anywhere.

--- Zig Ziglar.

Take a chance! All life is a chance. The man who goes further is generally the one who is willing to do and dare.

--- Dale Carnegie.

To be successful in business, be daring, be first, be different.

--- Merchant.

The boundary between the impossible and the extraordinary is extremely fine; life is a promise of adventure, often extraordinary, never impossible. Passion and fantasy can certainly result in excess, but if you have to choose between excess and immobility, don't hesitate. Always and everywhere you have to dare.

--- *Bernard Tapie.*

Only those who dare to fail greatly can ever achieve greatly.

--- *Robert F. Kennedy.*

DEFEAT

No one ever is defeated until defeat has been accepted as a reality.

--- *Napoleon Hill.*

You are not defeated unless you believe you are.

--- *Fernando.*

The deepest personal defeat is constituted by the difference between what one has become and what one would be capable of becoming.

--- Ashley Montagne.

DELAY

My guiding principle has been to avoid putting things off for tomorrow.

--- Duke of Wellington.

Have you ever noticed that the longer you put off something you should do, the more difficult it is to get started?

--- *Earl Nightingale.*

DELEGATION

Highly placed individuals who succeed best sort their tasks with the greatest care. They don't try and do everything themselves. They know how to develop and cultivate confidence. In this way they are free to think and plan. They have time to make important calls, and to meet worthwhile people.

--- B. C. Forbes.

When in charge, meditate. When in doubt, mumble. When in difficulty, delegate.

--- *Anonymous.*

DESIRE

He who really wants glory ends up by getting it, or at least coming very close. But you have to want it, and not only once, you have to want it each moment.

--- *Marie-Jean H. De Sechelles.*

A man who wants something so much that he is capable of risking his entire future on a simple throw of the dice in order to get it, is sure to succeed.

--- *Napoleon Hill.*

Being superior to others has never required great effort. What is difficult is the desire to be superior to yourself.

--- *Claude Debussy.*

Anybody can wish for riches, and most people do, but only a few know that a definite plan, plus a burning desire for wealth, are the only dependable means of accumulating wealth.

--- Napoleon Hill.

I believe in the power of desire backed by faith, because I have seen this power lift men from lowly beginnings to places of power and wealth.

--- Napoleon.

What you ardently and constantly desire, you always get.

--- Napoleon.

DESTINY

Sow a thought and you reap an act; sow an act and you reap a habit; sow a habit and you reap a character; sow a character and you reap a destiny.

--- Ralph W. Emerson.

Destiny is not a matter of chance, it is a matter of choice; it isn't a thing to be waited for, it is a thing to be achieved.

--- *W. J. Byran.*

A man's destiny is determined by what he thinks of himself.

--- *H. D. Thoreau.*

Our victory and our loss lie within ourselves.

--- *Epictetus.*

Lots of folks confuse bad management with destiny.

--- Frank M. Hubboard.

DETAILS

A handful of men have become very rich simply by paying attention to details that most others ignored.

---Henry Ford.

Whoever wants to accomplish great things must devote a lot of profound thought to details.

--- *Paul Valery.*

I would never have succeeded in life, if I hadn't given the same care and attention to the small things as I did to the big.

--- *Charles Dickens.*

DETERMINATION

When Churchill learned of this he made a decision: the Bismarck had to be sunk. His staff officers advised him this couldn't be done. The logic of the moment showed the British obviously lacked ships, aircraft, and fire power to do the job..... But all the negative talk didn't discourage Churchill. He was determined .... Churchill closed all the escape hatches. He was 100 percent committed to sinking the Bismarck. And it was sunk.

--- *Dr. D. J. Schwartz.*

Some men succeed because they are destined to, but most men because they are determined to.

--- *Zig Ziglar.*

We will either find a way or make one.

--- *Hannibal.*

DIRECTION

I find the great thing in this world is not so much where we stand, as in what direction we are moving.

--- Oliver Wendell Holmes.

DISCIPLINE

Discipline is the soul of an army. It makes small numbers formidable, procures success to the weak, and esteem to all.

--- George Washington.

The discipline of writing something down is the first step toward making it happen.

--- Lee Iacocca.

The discipline you impose on yourself by writing things down is the first step towards getting them done.

--- Lee Iacocca.

DOING GOOD

He that does good to another does also good to himself; not only in the consequence, but in the very act of doing it; for the consciousness of well-doing is an ample reward.

--- *Seneca.*

DOUBTS

Anything you become involved with must be worth your total commitment. Going into a venture with large doubts is writing a script for its failure.

--- *Victor Kiam.*

DREAMS

I've always believed that if you stick to a thought and carefully avoid distraction along the way, you can fulfill a dream. My whole life has been about fulfilling dreams. I kept my eye on the target, whatever that target was. Anyone who wants to achieve a dream must stay strong, focused and steady.

--- Estee Lauder.

All big men are dreamers. They see things in the soft haze of a spring day or in the red fire of a long winter's evening. Some of us let great dreams die, but others nourish and protect them, nurse them through bad days till they bring them to the sunshine and light which comes always to those who sincerely hope that their dreams will come true.

--- Woodrow Wilson.

Each man should frame life so that at some future hour facts and his dreamings meet.

--- Victor Hugo.

All men who have achieved great things have been dreamers.

--- O. S. Marden.

We need men who can dream of things that never were.

--- John F. Kennedy.

If you can dream it, you can do it.

--- *Walt Disney.*

EFFORTS

All occupations have a big money promise if you (a) really like it, and (b) give it the maximum effort.

--- *Dr. D. J. Schwartz.*

EGO

There must be no over-inflation of the ego in the direction of 'egomania' by which some men destroy themselves .... Striking examples of such men are Adolf Hitler, Benito Mussolini and the Kaiser, ... When men begin to thirst for control over others, or begin to accumulate large sums of money which they cannot or do not use constructively, they are treading upon dangerous grounds.

--- Napoleon Hill.

Strong, vital egos cannot be developed by dwelling on thought of past unpleasant experiences. Vital egos thrive on the hopes and desires of the yet unattained objective.

--- Napoleon Hill.

EMPOWERING

We can empower other people with a minimum amount of effort on our part. In doing so, we strengthen both ourselves and the other person.

--- John Kehoe.

ENERGY

A man can be a star of the first magnitude in gifts, will-power and endurance, but so well balanced that he turns with the system to which he belongs without any friction or waste of energy. Another may have the same great gifts, or even finer ones, but the axis does not pass precisely through the centre and he squanders half his strength in eccentric movements which weaken him and disturb his surroundings.

--- Hermann Hesse.

Self-motivated action occurs only when you have a pool of energy to draw from. Therefore, your success will depend on your health, your fitness, your mental well being, and amount of rest you get.

--- *George Shinn.*

There is no genius in life like the genius of energy and industry.

--- *Mitchell.*

Energy and perseverance can fit a man for almost any kind of position.

--Theodore F. Merseles.

The world belongs to the energetic.

--- Emerson.

ENJOYMENT

There are two things to aim at in life: first, to get what you want; and after that, to enjoy it. Only the wisest of mankind achieve the second.

--- Logan Pearsall Smith.

ENTERPRISE

How do you build a business that can compete not only within a country but on a global basis? We first start with a tight and firmly fastened focus on our ultimate customer. Next, we cultivated in our company a culture founded on organized orderliness. Third, we nurture in our company a passion for quality, a determination that every product we produce will be and will do for every customer what he bought it for. Fourth, we develop in every one of our people an abhorrence of waste - the waste of manpower, the waste of raw materials, the waste of space, the waste of machine time. Fifth, we empower our people to excellently accomplish the business of our business. Sixth, we rely on teams rather than on individuals to get things done. Finally, we cultivate in our company a spirit of "divine discontent"....... It can always be done better. It should always be improved.

--- G. A. Mendoza.

The secret of business is to know something that nobody else knows.

--- Aristotle S. Onassis.

If you don't drive your business, you will be driven out of business.

--- B. C. Forbes.

Buy low, sell high, deposit quickly and pay late is the secret of good business.

--- Dick Levin.

ENTHUSIASM

Our human nature seems to be such that we actually function more smoothly and more happily when we are active, questing, challenging, stimulated. When we go out of our way to expand our interests and our knowledge we gain a sense of satisfaction; when we narrow our interests and cease to grow, we feel dissatisfied.

--- Professor James C. Coleman.

The worst bankruptcy in the world is the man who has lost his enthusiasm. Let a man lose everything else in the world but his enthusiasm and he will come through again to success.

--- H. W. Arnold.

The great accomplishments of man have resulted from the transmission of ideas and enthusiam.

--- Thomas J. Watson.

The Greeks gave us the most beautiful word in our language: The word 'enthusiasm' - from the Greek En Thev which means 'inner God.!

--- *Louis Pasteur.*

Do you know anyone who is zealous in their work? He is the equal of kings.

--- *John Rockefeller.*

Enthusiasm is the greatest asset in the world. It beats money and power and influence.

--- Henry Chester.

If you are not getting as much from life as you want to, then examine the state of your enthusiasm.

--- Norman Vincent Peale.

Zest is the secret of all beauty. There is no beauty that is attractive without zest.

--- Christian Dior.

Experience shows that success is due less to ability than to zeal. The winner is he who gives himself to his work, body and soul.

--- Charles Buxton.

Nothing great was ever achieved without enthusiasm.

--- R. W. Emerson.

An enthusiast is a fanatic about life. And because the enthusiast has the attitude that good things will happen, good things do happen.

--- George Shinn..

Enthusiasm without knowledge is no good; impatience will get you into trouble.

--- Proverb 19:2

The person who loves always becomes enthusiastic.

--- Norman V. Peale.

Act enthusiastic and you became enthusiastic.

--- Dale Carnegie.

You can do anything if you have enthusiasm..... Enthusiasm is at the bottom of all progress. With it, there is accomplishment. Without it, there are only alibis.

--- Henry Ford.

No man who is enthusiastic about his work has anything to fear from life.

--- Samuel Goldwyn.

A positive attitude triggers enthusiasm.

--- Elwood N. Chapman.

Every production of genius must be the production of enthusiasm.

--- Disraeli.

Every great and commanding movement in the annals of the world is the triumph of enthusiasm. Nothing great was ever achieved without it.

--- Emerson.

You can do nothing effectually without enthusiasm.

--- Guizot.

ENVIRONMENT

You are subject to your environment. Therefore, select the environment that will best develop you toward your desired objective.

--- *W. Clement Stone.*

EQUILIBRIUM

When everything has its proper place in our mind, we are able to stand in equilibrium with the rest of the world.

--- Frederic Amiel.

EXCEL

Few people dare get into business because, deep down, they say to themselves: 'Why should I put such and such a product on the market when somebody else is producing it already? As for me, I've always said: 'Why not do better? And that's what I did'.

--- Henry Ford.

EXCELLENCE

Give the best to the world and the best will come to you.

--- Anonymous.

No man fails who does his best.

--- O. S. Marden.

Any executive worth the title prefers dealing with people who aim too high than those who are timid.

--- Lee Iacocca.

It's a funny thing about life; if you refuse to accept anything but the best, you very often get it.

--- W. S. Maugham.

I love those who reach for the impossible.

--- Goethe.

When you think you've given it all you've got to, remember: your best can always be made better.

--- George Shinn.

The talent of success is nothing more than doing what you can do well, and doing well whatever you do ....

--- *Longfellow.*

We are best when we are doing our best. And to do one's best, it can never be good enough to strive for 50% or 75%.

--- *Mark H. McCormack.*

If you consistently do your best, the worst won't happen.

--- *B. C. Forbes.*

Management consists of showing average people how to produce superior work.

--- John Rockefeller.

Whatever is worth doing is worth doing well.

--- P. D. Stanhope.

EXCUSE

Fear is never a reason for quitting: it is only an excuse.

--- Norman Vincent Peale.

If you want to do something, you find a way. If you don't want to do anything, you find an excuse.

--- Anonymous.

EXERCISE

Do enough exercise and keep yourself in shape. Practising basic yoga is recommended both for the body and the mind. If you can do Judo for an hour or two a week, you can get rid of all your complexes.

--- Aristotle Onassis.

All managers should know to what extent physical exercise, practised hard, is good not only for the heart, but also for mind; it gives you a calm sense of confidence in yourself. And having self-confidence is very important.

--- *Akiko Morita.*

EXPERIENCE

When a person with experience meets a person with money, pretty soon the person with the experience will have the money, and the person with the money will have the experience.

--- Estee Lauder.

My experience with people is that they generally do what you expect them to do! If you expect them to perform well, they will. Conversely, if you expect them to perform poorly, they'll probably oblige.

--- *Mary Kay Ash.*

Experience is a hard teacher because she gives the test first, the lesson afterwards.

--- *V. S. Law*

The art of living is the art of using experience, your own and other people's.

--- Viscount Samuel.

Experience is the most efficient tool for transforming innovation into action.

--- Peter Peterson.

EXPERTISE

We should concentrate on the things we know best.

--- *Arthur Spear.*

FAILURE

Never walk away from failure. On the contrary, study it carefully and imaginatively – for it's hidden assets.

--- *Michael Korda.*

There is no safe way to be a good leader. You do not win all the time and you have to learn that failure is part of the leadership game – so long as you don't make the same mistake twice.

--- *Sir Colin Marshall.*

Each time I met with failure, I analysed it and always noticed, looking back, that I had ignored an essential aspect of the problem because it had seemed unimportant.

--- *Bernard Tapie.*

Failure is the opportunity to begin again more intelligently.

--- Henry Ford.

I think that each of the failures I had to face provided me with the opportunity of starting again and trying something new.

--- Colonel Sanders, Kentucky Fried Chicken.

Coping with adversity is necessary for achieving a successful career. Learning how to prepare for career downturns and how to manage them is part of climbing the corporate ladder. Resilient people have an inner strength of character that colours their perception of adverse circumstances. Successful executives reveal that they don't even think about failure and don't even use the word. Instead, they rely on synonyms such as 'mistake', 'bungle' and 'setback'.

--- *Andrew J. Dubrin.*

FANTASY

Successful people are able to entertain fantasies, then carry them into reality.

--- Michael Korda.

FATE

Whatever fate befalls you, do not give way to great rejoicing or great lamentation .... All things are full of change, and your fortunes may turn at any moment.

--- Arthur Schopenhauer.

When fate is adverse, a wise man can always strive for happiness and sail against the wind to attain it.

--- Rousseau.

FEAR

I fear nothing. Least of all do I fear being afraid. I know there is no such thing as fear. I know there is reasonable sense of precaution, care, and common sense. I see everything in its correct perspective and right proportion. This being so, I have no need of fear.

--- *Dr. Gilbert Oakley.*

Very often a fear is due to using your mind more than your body. There should be balance. You generate fears if you think too much and neglect action. Lead a more active life, exercise in the open, go for long walks.

--- Al Koran.

There can be no security where there is fear.

--- Felix Frankfurter.

He who fears being conquered is sure of defeat.

--- Napoleon.

Fear is the main source of superstition, and one of the main sources of cruelty. To conquer fear is the beginning of wisdom.

--- *Bertrand Russell.*

A man without fear succeeds in everything he undertakes.

--- *Napoleon Hill.*

Fears are easy to throw away once you put them in their proper perspective. If you analyze them, you'll often find that they're really silly and immaterial, and the vast majority don't even exist except in your mind.

--- *Robert L. Shook.*

FELLOW MEN

William James once remarked that those who are concerned with making the world more healthy had best start with themselves. We could go further and point out that finding the centre of strength within ourselves is in the long run the best contribution we can make to our fellow men.

--- Dr. Rollo May.

I believe it is my duty to make money, and still more money, and to use the money I make for the good of my fellow men according to the dictates of my conscience.

--- John Rockfeller.

FIRST IMPRESSION

You get only one chance to make a first impression.

--- R. L. Shook.

FOCUS

All that you dream of, all that you yearn for and long to be, will be within your reach if you have the power to affirm sufficiently strong, if you can focus your faculties with sufficient intentness on a single purpose.

--- *O S. Marden.*

FORGIVENESS

Forgiveness is the key to action and freedom.

--- Hannah Arendt.

To be wronged is nothing unless you continue to remember it.

--- Confucius.

Joy to forgive, and joy to the forgiven hand level in the balance of love.

--- Richard Garrett.

There are times when forgetting can be just as important as remembering - and even more difficult.

--- Harry Mier.

FORTUNES

From studying hundreds of cases of people who have made large fortunes, it became apparent that these people were in the habit of making very rapid decisions, and of changing their minds with reluctance.

--- Napoleon Hill.

FREEDOM

Remember that thoughts and spoken words are things. Proclaim the news of your joy and be free, completely free of all limitation. Then know that you are free, and triumphantly pursue your chosen path in total freedom.

--- B. T. Spalding.

That man is truly free who desires what he is able to perform, and does what he desires.

--- Rousseau.

FRIENDSHIP

A faithful friend is the medicine of life.

--- Ecclesiasticus 6:16.

Life is to be fortified by many friendships. To love and be loved is the greatest happiness of existence.

--- *Sydney Smith.*

A friend is a present you give yourself.

--- *R. L. Stevenson.*

My best friend is the one who brings out the best in me.

--- *Henry Ford.*

A man who turns his back on his friends soon finds himself facing a very small audience.

--- *Dick Powell.*

Am I not destroying my enemies when I make friends of them?

--- *Abraham Lincoln.*

This communicating of a man's self to his friend works two contrary effect; for it redoubleth joys, and cutteth griefs in half.

--- *Francis Bacon.*

The more you live to help others in the overcoming of their obstacles, the more certain you are of solving your own ..... Friendship brings out the magic .... Suddenly you meet someone, and you know instinctively he or she is your kind of person ... Let us try to keep what friends we have, for what a treasure beyond compare it is to have at least one friend who has been with us throughout a lifetime.

--- Al Koran.

Without real friends even a millionaire is poor.

--- Forbes.

One is never poor, even though his clothes may be worn and his purse empty, if he still has the love and understanding of loyal friends.

--- Buford Ellington.

Radiate friendship and it will be returned tenfold.

--- H. P. Davidson.

If a man is worth knowing at all, he is worth knowing well.

--- Alexander Smith.

FUTURE

Man has his future within him, dynamically alive at this present moment.

--- Abraham Maslow.

You are free to choose, but the choices you make today will determine what you will have, be, and do in the tomorrows of your life.

--- Zig Ziglar.

GENEROSITY

No one can become rich without enriching others. Anyone who adds to his prosperity must prosper others in turn.

--- G. Alexander Orndorff.

No man who continues to add something to the material, intellectual, and moral well-being of the place in which he lives is left long without proper reward.

--- Booker T. Washington.

It seems odd but it is correct. Put giving first and getting takes care of itself. The generous prosper. The selfish don't. You can rely on this as a general rule: prosperity varies in proportion to generosity.

--- Anonymous.

I wanted to help people. At the time of the W. P. A. I aided a number of families, even though I was poor myself. I have always given money to the church, and supported religious work.

--- *Colonel Sanders of Kentucky Fried Chicken.*

GIVING

Those who bring sunshine into the lives of others cannot keep it from themselves.

--- *J. M. Barrie.*

You give but little when you give of your possessions. It is when you give of yourself that you truly give.

--- Gibran.

Give what you have. To some it may be better than you dare think.

--- Longfellow.

Whatever you give comes back to you.

--- Estee Lauder.

GLORY

Glory is given only to those who have always dreamed of it.

--- Charles de Gaulle.

GOALS

All successful people have a goal. No one can get anywhere unless he knows where he wants to go and what he wants to be or do.

--- Norman V. Peale.

This one step – choosing a goal and sticking to it – changes everything.

--- *Scott Reid.*

Condition yourself to determine clearly in your mind the goal that you want to achieve, and then, without letting yourself get side-tracked, head straight for your ideal.

--- *Dale Carnegie.*

Decide what you want, decide what you are willing to exchange for it. Establish your priorities and go to work!

--- *H. L. Hunt.*

Better get a stiff neck for aiming too high than a hunch back for aiming too low.

--- *Jacques Chancel.*

You read a book from the beginning to the end. You run a business the opposite way. You start with the end, and then you do everything you must to reach it. The beauty of setting a realistic objective - or as I said, starting out with the end - is that the goal itself will begin to define what it is you have to do to attain it.

--- Harold Geneen, President, AT & T.

To become a billionaire, you have to have the mentality of a billionaire. This particular state of mind concentrates all knowledge and intelligence on a single and unique goal.

--- John Paul Getty, American Billionaire.

You must have long-range goals to keep you from being frustrated by short-range failure.

--- Charles Noble.

is not enough to take steps that might one day lead to a goal; ach step should, in itself, be a goal, and at the same time, carry s closer to the greater goal.

--- *Goethe.*

nowing your destination is half the journey.

--- *Anonymous.*

GRATITUDE

Remember the old expression, 'I felt sorry for myself because I had no shoes until I met a man who had no feet'. Sit down and count your blessings. You've got more than you think!

--- Dr D. J. Schwartz.

Do you know who the luckiest people on earth are? To my way of thinking, they are those who have developed an almost constant sense of gratitude.

--- E. Nightingale.

GREATNESS

Keep away from people who try to belittle your ambitions. Small people always do that. But the really great make you feel that you too can become great.

--- *Mark Twain.*

Integrity is the first step to true greatness.

--- *C. Simmons*

Real greatness consists of being master of yourself.

--- Daniel Defoe.

The difference between great and good is a little extra effort.

--- Clarence Munn.

There is a great man, who makes every man feel small. But the real great man is the man who makes every man feel great.

--- G. K. Chesteron.

My experience has taught me that the next best thing to being truly great is to emulate the great, in feeling and action, as closely as possible.

--- *Napoleon Hill.*

The characteristic of a great man is his power to leave a lasting impression on the people he meets.

--- *Winston Churchill.*

The greatness of human actions is measured by the extent to which they inspire others.

--- *Louis Pasteur.*

GROWTH

You grow up the day you have the first real laugh - at yourself.

--- *Ethel Barrymore.*

The self-motivator has a thirst for growth. He or she realizes that growth means change and change involves risks, stepping from the known to the unknown.

--- George Shinn.

INDEX

Ability	1	Challenge	25
Achievement	1	Champions	27
Action	5	Change	28
Activity	8	Character	29
Adaptability	9	Children, Childhood	32
Advice	11	Circumstances	33
Aloofness	11	Colleagues	35
Alternatives	12	Colours	36
Appearance	13	Communications	37
Appreciation	13	Contentment	37
Aspiration	14	Conversation	38
Assumption	15	Co-operation	40
Attitude	15	Confidence	42
Beauty	18	Company	45
Beginning	18	Concentration	46
Belief	19	Courage	48
Blame	20	Courtesy	53
Brain	21	Creativity	55
Career	22	Daring	57
Catalyst	23	Defeat	60
Cause & Effect	23	Delay	61
Caution	24	Delegation	63

INDEX

Desire	64	Experience	107
Destiny	67	Expertise	110
Details	69	Failure	110
Determination	71	Fantasy	114
Direction	73	Fate	115
Discipline	73	Fear	116
Doing Good	75	Fellow Men	120
Doubts	76	First Impression	121
Dreams	77	Focus	122
Efforts	80	Forgiveness	123
Ego	81	Fortunes	124
Empowering	82	Freedom	125
Energy	83	Friendship	126
Enjoyment	86	Future	131
Enterprise	87	Generosity	132
Enthusiasm	89	Giving	134
Environment	98	Glory	136
Equilibrium	99	Goals	136
Excel	100	Gratitude	142
Excellence	101	Greatness	143
Excuse	104	Growth	146
Exercise	105		